TRUMPET

GREAT JAZZ

CONTENTS

ISBN 0-7935-4916-7

HAL•LEONARD®
CORPORATION

7777 W. BLUEMOUND RD. P.O. BOX 13819 MILWAUKEE, WI 53213

Visit Hal Leonard Online at
www.halleonard.com

ALFIE
Theme from the Paramount Picture ALFIE

Trumpet

Words by HAL DAVID
Music by BURT BACHARACH

ALL OF ME

Trumpet

Words and Music by SEYMOUR SIMONS
and GERALD MARKS

APRIL IN PARIS

Trumpet

Words by E.Y. HARBURG
Music by VERNON DUKE

BLUE SKIES

Trumpet

Words and Music by
IRVING BERLIN

CARAVAN
from SOPHISTICATED LADIES

Trumpet

Words and Music by DUKE ELLINGTON,
IRVING MILLS and JUAN TIZOL

DARN THAT DREAM

Trumpet

Lyric by EDDIE DE LANGE
Music by JIMMY VAN HEUSEN

IS IT TRUE WHAT THEY SAY ABOUT DIXIE

Trumpet

Words and Music by IRVING CAESAR,
SAMMY LERNER and GERALD MARKS

IT DON'T MEAN A THING
(If It Ain't Got That Swing)
from SOPHISTICATED LADIES

Trumpet

Words and Music by DUKE ELLINGTON
and IRVING MILLS

LET'S FALL IN LOVE

Trumpet

Words by TED KOEHLER
Music by HAROLD ARLEN

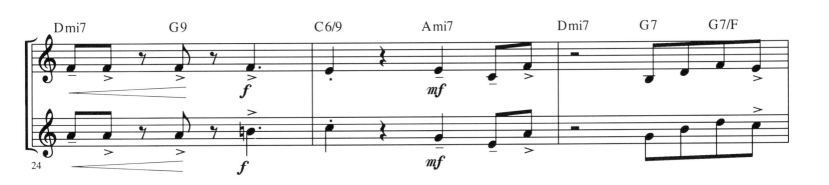

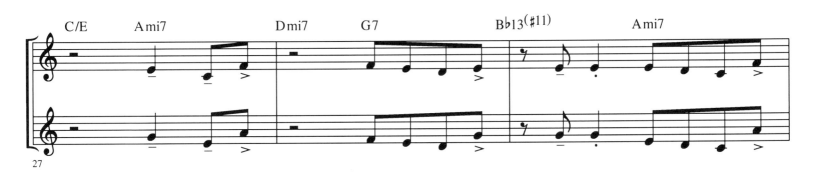

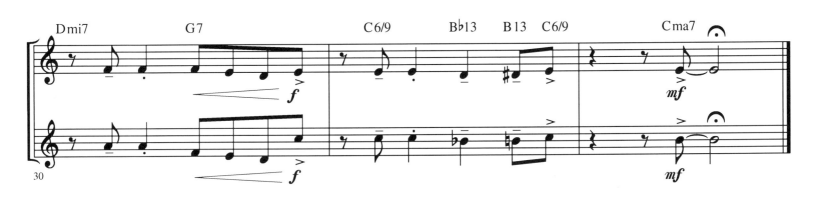

STAR DUST

Trumpet

Words by MITCHELL PARISH
Music by HOAGY CARMICHAEL

UNFORGETTABLE

Trumpet

Words and Music by
IRVING GORDON

WAVE

Trumpet

Words and Music by
ANTONIO CARLOS JOBIM

THE WAY YOU LOOK TONIGHT

from SWING TIME

Trumpet

Words by DOROTHY FIELDS
Music by JEROME KERN

WHEN SUNNY GETS BLUE

Trumpet

Lyric by JACK SEGAL
Music by MARVIN FISHER

WHEN YOU WISH UPON A STAR

Trumpet

Words by NED WASHINGTON
Music by LEIGH HARLINE